First published in The United States by **Holland Brown Books, LLC** 2010

The Green Building
732 East Market Street
Louisville
Kentucky 40202
USA
www.hollandbrownbooks.com

Copyright © 2010 Holland Brown Books
Manufactured by Friesens Corporation in Altona, MB, Canada (December, 2015)
D#218945

ISBN 13: 978-0-9797006-4-4
ISBN 10: 0-9797006-4-7
Library of Congress Control Number: 2010933542

L is for Louisville! A Children's Abecedary & Art Book
2nd Edition

Written by Gill Holland
Edited by Stephanie Brothers

Contributing Artists
Brook White, Vian Sora, Aron Conaway, David Schuster, Joyce Garner, Nana Lampton, Becky Freytag,
Sara Robinette, Denise Furnish, Cynthia Norton, Ron Jasin, Lori Beck, Lucy Brown, Jason Pierce, Gwendolyn Kelly,
Michael Brohm, Chuck Swanson, Valerie White, Hallie Jones, Ty Kreft, David Mahoney, Ngoc Phan,
John Begley, Kathleen Lolley, Geoff Carr, Clare Hirn, Christy Zurkuhlen.

Supplementary Photography by Kertis Creative, LLC
Graphic Design by Ty Kreft
Cover Illustration by Amanda Joyce Bishop

Typeset and Printed in Canada.

For Cora,
Owsley, and Lilla

L is for LOUISVILLE!

A Children's Abecedary & Art Book

written by **Gill Holland**

edited by **Stephanie Brothers**

With generous contribution from 27 fantastic
LOUISVILLE ARTISTS:

Brook White, Vian Sora, Aron Conaway, David Schuster, Joyce Garner, Nana Lampton, Becky Freytag, Sara Robinette, Denise Furnish, Cynthia Norton, Ron Jasin, Lori Beck, Lucy Brown, Jason Pierce, Gwendolyn Kelly, Michael Brohm, Chuck Swanson, Valerie White, Hallie Jones, Ty Kreft, David Mahoney, Ngoc Phan, John Begley, Kathleen Lolley, Geoff Carr, Clare Hirn, Christy Zurkuhlen.

A is for ALI CENTER.

The mission of the Muhammad Ali Center is to preserve and share the legacy and ideals of Muhammad Ali, to promote respect, hope, and understanding, and to inspire adults and children everywhere to be as great as they can be.

B is for BELLE OF LOUISVILLE,

the oldest original paddle-boat still in operation. Also called a steamboat, the Belle is a National Historic Landmark.

C is for GENERAL GEORGE ROGERS CLARK,

the founder of Louisville in 1778. His brother William was half of the famous explorer team Lewis and Clark. He is buried in Cave Hill Cemetery.

D is for

DERBY.

The Kentucky Derby is the most famous horse race in the world. It is called "the most exciting two minutes in sports"!

E is for EXTREME.

The Louisville Extreme Park has over 40,000 feet devoted to skateboarding, biking and fun.

F is for FALLS OF THE OHIO.

These 386-million-year-old fossil beds are among the largest naturally-exposed coral beds in the world. Can you imagine that Louisville used to be under the ocean?

G is for GUM.

Did you know John Colgan from Louisville invented chewing gum in 1879?

H is for HORSES.

Many consider Kentucky's grassy farms the best place in the world to breed and raise horses. Their bones are strong from the good water filtering through our limestone.

I is for IDEA FESTIVAL.

We think Louisville's festival to celebrate and listen to ideas from around the world is a great idea!

$$v = \lim_{\Delta t \to 0} x \; \frac{x(t + \Delta t) - x(t)}{\Delta t} = \frac{dx}{dt}$$

J is for JUG BAND.

Earl McDonald started the first Louisville jug band over 100 years ago, making music from bourbon jugs!

K is for KENTUCKY!

Did you know the early settlers called it Cantuckee after the Wyandot Indian tribe's word Ken-tah-teh, meaning "Land of Tomorrow"?

L is for...

I bet you **know** the answer to this one!

LOUISVILLE!

The coolest city in America. Home sweet home! Louisville was named after French King Louis XVI. We've hidden 16 Louisville icons here. Can you find them all?

SEE PAGE 58 FOR THE ANSWERS!

L is for LOUIS' VILLE

M is for MADOC.

Do you know the oldest American legend of Prince Madoc of Wales? Many people believe he came to the Louisville area in 1170, over 300 years before Christopher Columbus, and 100 years after Leif Ericson the Viking first discovered North America.

The Beautiful River
(Ohio River)

Wiggins Point Fortress

X Falls of the Ohio

The Dark and Forbidden Land

Acuzamil
(America)

"The Land of Gwynedd"
(Wales)

Great Western Sea
(Atlantic Ocean)

The Gwenan Gorn
(Prince Madoc's Ship)

M

N
E
W
S

Not to Scale

ca 1170 a.d.

N is for NULU.

NuLu is the arts district of Louisville where you can find lots of art and many of the artists who made this book. Louisville is the "City of Arts and Parks"™.

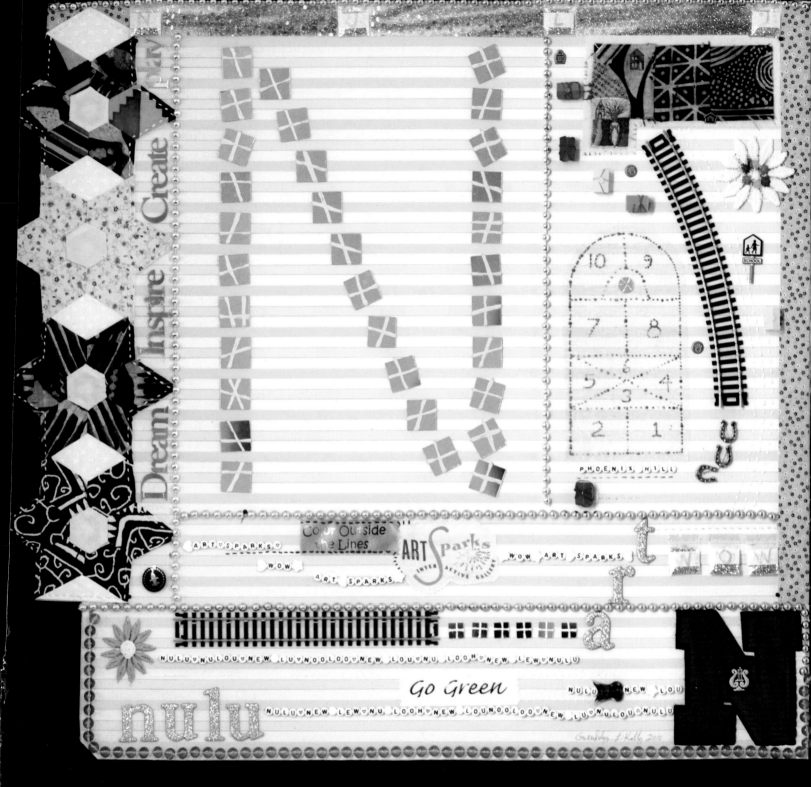

O is for OHIO RIVER.

Did you know over one million gallons of water flow by every minute? The river is wide and deep here in Louisville.

Pis for PARKS.

Louisville has 122 parks on 14,000 acres where you can play! Remember? Louisville is the "City of Arts and Parks"™.

Q is for QUILT.

Quilts matter to Louisville. We are a patchwork quilt of different people, customs and faiths. Did you know that the "Quilt Index" started in Louisville in 1992 and now you can see 50,000 quilts online?

R is for ROSES.

Did you know there are over 500 roses in the garland given to the horse that wins the Kentucky Derby? This is why it is called "The Run for the Roses".

S is for COLONEL SANDERS.

He started cooking at age 6 and came up with the secret recipe of 11 spices and herbs which now helps sell over one billion Kentucky Fried Chicken™ meals a year in over 80 countries.

T is for THEATRE.

The Humana Festival of New American Plays happens every spring at Actors Theatre of Louisville! It is the most famous new play festival in the world.

U is for UNIVERSITIES.

When you grow up and go to college, you can become a Cardinal at the University of Louisville or a Knight at Bellarmine University or a Golden Eagle at Spalding University.

Is For
Universities

V is for VICTORIAN HOUSES.

Louisville has the largest collection of Victorian houses in the United States. You can make a good ghost movie in Louisville!

W is for WFPK, WUOL and WFPL.

Did you know Louisville is the only city in America with three public radio stations under one roof? 91.9, 90.5, 89.3 on the FM dial!

X is for
XYLOPHONE,

one of the many instruments used in the famous Louisville Orchestra.

Y is for YOU!

You are a great artist and can make a work of art here!

→

Z is for ZACHARY TAYLOR.

He lived and is buried in Louisville. He was President of the United States, and you can be President one day too!

LOUISVILLE ARTISTS

Brooke White (A)

Owner of Flame Run, Brook Forrest White, Jr., discovered his passion for hot glass at Centre College in Danville, Kentucky. In 1995 he founded the studio, glassbrook, to experiment and further explore hot glass. He has worked with countless glass artists from around the world and garnered numerous awards and recognition in museums and galleries across the country.

Vian Sora (B)

Vian Sora was born in Baghdad, Iraq. She has lived in many places throughout the world, and moved to Louisville in 2009 from Dubai. Her work is character-driven with symbols and images that have hidden meaning. It comes from both her spiritually and her dreams – which are at times so vivid that in the light of day they come to life through her hand on canvas. She truly believes that art is not worth doing unless it attempts to touch us deeply and nudge us gently to remember our humanness and connection to one another.

Aron Conaway (C)

Aron Conaway is an independent curator, studio artist and freelancer born and raised in Louisville. He has a B.F.A. in Photography and M.A. in Critical and Curatorial Studies from the University of Louisville. He currently manages the Louisville Visual Art Association's Open Doors program and is part-time faculty at the Kentucky School of Art. In 2001, Aron co-founded the Louisville Assembly of Vanguard Art (LAVA) and in 2005, with wife Hallie Jones, purchased historic Nelligan Hall in the Portland Neighborhood, where they run a collective gallery and studios (near General George Rogers Clark's founding settlement in Louisville).

www.aronconaway.com

David Schuster (D)

David Schuster was born and raised in Louisville, where he received a solid foundation in visual art at Trinity High School. He continued his studies and began his professional career as an artist at the University of Virginia. He is now an accomplished painter, working in several genres including portraits, figurative, landscape, equine and mixed media. David has murals and paintings in both private and corporate collections across the country. He owns and operates David Schuster Fine Art, where he teaches, creates, and shows his art.

Joyce Garner (E)

Joyce Garner is a studio painter working large scale with oil on canvas. Her studio is open to the public at 642 East Market Street, NuLu.

www.thegarners.net/joyce

Nana Lampton (F)

Nana Lampton is a businesswoman, farmer, artist and poet. She is Chairman and CEO of Hardscuffle, Inc. and American Life and Accident Insurance Company of Kentucky and serves on boards including Constellation Energy, DNP Select Income Fund, Louisville's Downtown Development Corporation, Shakertown at Pleasant Hill, Bluegrass Conservancy, and Kentucky Historical Society. A graduate of Wellesley College (B.A.), University of Virginia (M.A.), and Spalding University (M.F.A), Ms. Lampton has published two books of poetry and frequently exhibits her oil and watercolor paintings in area art shows. She lives and farms in Goshen, Kentucky.

Becky Freytag (G)

A portrait photographer living in Louisville, Becky Freytag uses natural light and outdoor settings to create personal portraits of children.

Combining close working relationships with her clients with careful, methodical technical processes, Becky captures the expressions, personalities and spirits of her subjects. Energized and inspired by children, Becky taught Middle School for many years. During a period living in Laguna Beach, Becky brought together her love for art and appreciation for children by starting her own photography business. With a California influence that takes advantage of natural environments and available light, she produces candid, unique portraits of her subjects.

Sara Robinette (H)

Sara is a native Kentuckian, who journeyed many places before calling Louisville home. Running a commercial photography studio by day, she considers herself extremely lucky to be an employed creative. Beyond the camera, she dabbles in many other mediums. Sara is currently most fascinated with the culinary arts and observing how her garden grows.

LOUISVILLE ARTISTS

Denise Furnish (I)

Denise Mucci Furnish was born in Louisville, Kentucky. She has backgrounds in surface design and graphic design. She worked as a graphic designer for 16 years before devoting full time to fine art. The vernacular of antique quilts is the driving force behind her paintings. Her work has been exhibited internationally and has won awards in national exhibitions.

Cynthia Norton (J)

Cynthia Norton is a native of Kentucky, the environment where she has developed her artistic identity since early childhood. Norton relates sculptural and sonic interpretations of the domestic traditions of her Southern cultural heritage, creating video quilts, instruments, moonshine stills and kinetic dress sculptures. In 1995, while completing her M.F.A. at The Art Institute of Chicago in Time Arts, Norton developed her performance persona of Ninnie Naïve (based upon the classic country comedic genre of the "rube"; aka "Alternative Minnie Pearl", "a countryfied Laurie Anderson" and "a sarcastic hillbilly"). Currently Ninnie is "Ninnie; Ni'Mally," a budding musical naiad.

Ron Jasin (K)

Ron Jasin is a designer who specializes in Gig Posters and hand screened art. He has done work for a variety of artists including My Morning Jacket, The Decemberists, and Neil Young. Ron enjoys the structured freedom screen printing provides. He is also very fond of the physical quality of the process and the flux of it all. It allows him to be messy like a kid while he strives for perfection.

Lori Beck (L)

Born and raised in Louisville, Lori Beck is a graduate of the University of Louisville Fine Arts program, and also holds a Master's Degree in Curatorial Studies. Lori just opened her first business in the NuLu neighborhood: the Louisville Beer Store. She's a big fan of King Louis XVI and hopes everyone takes pride in our city and our city's namesake.

Lucy Brown (L)

Lucy Brown, born and raised in Louisville, will receive her B.F.A. from the University of Louisville in December 2010. Her studies have included drawing, printmaking, photography and digital media. To her, life is art, and beauty can be found in the simplest of moments. When not creating in the studio, she spends her time with her ever-growing pack of cats, dogs, birds and whoever else comes along.

Louisville icons on page 29 include a horse racing at Churchill Downs, a Louisville Stoneware Mug, a Cardinal bird, an Ear-x-tacy bumper sticker, boxing gloves, a Louisville Slugger Bat, a Thomas Edison Lightbulb, the Zachary Taylor Memorial, the Belle of Louisville Steamboat, a Cheeseburger, the Happy Birthday song, a bourbon bottle, a bucket of Kentucky Fried Chicken, the St. James Fountain, a map of the Falls of Ohio, and Thunder Over Louisville & the Ohio River Bridge. Did you find them all?

Jason Pierce (M)

Often working under the nom de plume MPERFECT design, Jason Pierce is a self-schooled graphic designer based in Louisville, Kentucky, who couldn't live without typewriters, records and other things analog.

Gwendolyn Kelly (N)

Gwendolyn Kelly was conceived in South Carolina but born/raised in Louisville. She learned to read at Dann C. Byck Elementary then attended McFerran and Noe Middle. She graduated from Ballard High School in 1981 (and still carries a grudge). She earned M.A. and B.F.A. degrees from UofL. She's been an artist since second grade when Mrs. Mattie White taught her to crochet. Gwen has work included in Fiberarts Design Books Six and Seven. She's lived in the California neighborhood since 1991. She loves reading and walking with her dog, M.A.G. (Magnificent Animal Girl).

www.MultiPurposeWoman.com.

Michael Brohm (O)

Michael Brohm is a photographer with 30 years experience in stills, film and video. He travels widely in the U.S. and abroad, is a writer and an avid outdoorsman. He is a portraitist of people and society and a photo educator. His current project is a book of portraits recalling the Cold War, shot in Perm, Russia.

Chuck Swanson (P)

Chuck Swanson was born in Wausau, Wisconsin and moved to Louisville as a child. He was the class "go to guy" for art projects throughout his school years but earned his college degree in Social Theory and Urban Sociology. Later he attended the Center for Photographic Studies and studied ceramics for over eight years. He opened Swanson Gallery

LOUISVILLE ARTISTS

in the 1980's near his home in the Highlands. In 1998 he opened what is now Swanson Reed Contemporary on East Market Street. He is married and has a nearly grown-up son who is a multi-instrumentalist and songwriter currently living in New York City.

Valerie White (Q)

Valerie C. White has been creating quilts for almost 20 years. She shares her passion for textiles by teaching and presenting lectures nationally. Her work appears in several publications and can be found in private collections around the world.

She received a B.F.A. from Howard University in Washington, DC and a M.A. from Virginia Polytechnic University in Blacksburg, Virginia. She taught Art and Humanities at the prestigious Paul Laurence Dunbar High School and retired as a Middle School Guidance Counselor from the District of Columbia School System in 1998. Since retirement she has been able to focus on creating art and supports a variety of community activities.

Valerie is married and has three adult children and two grandchildren.

Hallie Jones (R)

Hallie is the Director of Marketing and Communications at the Center For Neighborhoods, where she manages the PAINT Program (Producing Art In Neighborhoods Together), a neighborhood-based public art program. She was a member of the former LAVA House (Louisville Assembly of Vanguard Art) for six years and is a recipient

of a Kentucky Foundation for Women Artist Enrichment Grant. Her work has been exhibited at the Speed Art Museum and various galleries in Louisville and New York, and has been acquired by several private art collections including Deutsche Bank and Maker's Mark. She and her husband (Aron Conaway) are the owners of Nelligan Hall in the Portland neighborhood, an old Democratic social hall they converted into an artist collective studio and gallery space. She is currently earning her Masters of Art in Teaching K-12 Art Education (M.A.T.) at the University of Louisville. She is entering Indiana University at Bloomington in the fall as a Doctoral candidate in Art Education.

www.halliejones.com

Ty Kreft (S)

Ty Kreft is an award winning graphic artist working in Louisville, Kentucky. See his work at www.ajbmtk.com.

David Mahoney (T)

Mahoney was bred in Kentucky and studied under Tom Marsh for his M.A. in Ceramics at UofL. He has worked part-time as designer of new products at Louisville Stoneware for the last fifteen years.

Ngoc Phan (T)

Growing up in Hue City, Vietnam, from an early age, Ngoc Phan developed a love of art. A self-taught artist, he also earned a degree in civil engineering and architecture. He lives

in Kentucky and works as a senior designer for Louisville Stoneware. In the past 30 years he has developed his own unique style by combining Eastern and Western art. He has designed ceramics for the White House and Buckingham Palace. He currently has work on display at Buckingham Palace, where he received a silver award.

John Begley (U)

Louisville artist, curator and gallery director, John Begley (B.F.A. with Distinction, University of New Mexico, 1969; M.F.A., Indiana University, 1975) currently heads the University of Louisville's Hite Art Institute galleries and leads its Critical and Curatorial Studies program. The founding director of the New Harmony Gallery of Contemporary Art and an eighteen-year director of the Louisville Visual Art Association, Begley has produced hundreds of exhibitions worldwide.

A recipient of Louis Comfort Tiffany and Getty Museum Management Institute Fellowships, Begley oversaw the growth the Art Association from a five-member staff to a multi-function exhibition, education and advocacy art center with numerous art, community and corporate partners and over a million dollar budget. He has been an active advocate for the visual arts in Louisville, helping found co-operative galleries (Zephyr), organize an city-wide art dealers and presenters organization (LOOK) and work long-term for the establishment of a city public art program (MCOPA). He also serves on numerous community and regional arts advisory boards and panels as well as being an adjudicator for state, regional and

LOUISVILLE ARTISTS

national arts granting agencies including the IMLS.

In addition to directing the University of Louisville Hite galleries beginning in 2001 and expanding its facilities with a renovated Belknap campus gallery and new downtown gallery, the Cressman Center, he has mentored over twenty-five Curatorial Studies students.

Kathleen Lolley (V)

Kathleen Lolley spent her childhood split between Louisville and Pittsburgh, Pennsylvania. She attended California Institute of the Arts and received a B.F.A. in Experimental Animation. Storytelling plays a prominent role in her work. Her subject matter usually consists of critters trying to break the spell of day-to-day heartbreak. Lolley currently resides in Kentucky where she spends her time making crafts, comics and fine art.

Geoff Carr (W)

Geoff Carr has been a commercial photographer for the past 25 years and has won numerous awards locally and nationally. He studied at Louisville's Center for Photographic Studies from 1974–76 and earned a B.A. from the University of Louisville and a M.F.A. in photography from the University of Illinois Chicago.

He has pursued his own fine art work for several years. His studio is located in downtown Louisville at 221 Hancock Street and takes part in the First Friday Gallery Hop that occurs each month.

www.carr-photo.com

Clare Hirn (X)

Clare Hirn, a native of Louisville, Kentucky, received her undergraduate degree from Indiana University in Bloomington and her Masters in Painting and Drawing from the New York Academy of Art - Graduate School of Figurative Art.

After graduating in 1990, Clare worked for a mural design firm in NYC, learning the techniques of working large scale. She returned to Louisville in the mid 90's and, believing firmly in the value and power of regional arts, has participated and received awards in many regional shows and has had three one-person gallery shows. Her paintings and murals are in many private and public collections, homes and businesses and have appeared in numerous publications.

She is presently showing and working out of her studio in downtown Louisville.

Currently Clare is moving more into the world of public art. She recently installed murals in the UofL Outpatient Care facility and co-developed a project, funded by the Kentucky Foundation for Women, using art and experiential activities to explore the theme of healthy food and sustainable agriculture.

Christy Zurkuhlen (Z)

Christy Zurkuhlen, a Kentucky native, has been painting for 25 years. She is known in the Kentucky area for her poignant pastels and oil paintings of children and jockeys. Her specialty is portraits, equine, and trompe l'oeil. She studied art at the University of Louisville and the Schrodt School of Art.

Christy has recently established the Christy Zurkuhlen Gallery and Studio at 4820 Brownsboro Center. She is a member of the Portrait Society of America and is also the Ambassador for the State of Kentucky for the Portrait Society of America. She has recently established a local chapter in Kentucky. Kentucky Educational television featured her in a segment on "The Portrait Art of Christy Zurkuhlen."

Currently, Christy resides in Goshen, Kentucky, with her husband and her two children, Dane and Priscilla.

Thanks

to everyone who played a part in the making of *L is for Louisville!*

Thanks

to everyone who played a part in
the making of *L is for Louisville!*